BIG TOP ACADEMY

Tamsyn Murray

Illustrated by
Adriana Puglisi

OXFORD
UNIVERSITY PRESS

Great Clarendon Street, Oxford, OX2 6DP,
United Kingdom

Oxford University Press is a department of the University of Oxford.
It furthers the University's objective of excellence in research, scholarship,
and education by publishing worldwide. Oxford is a registered trade mark of
Oxford University Press in the UK and in certain other countries

British Library Cataloguing in Publication Data
Data available

978-0-19-837761-0

1 3 5 7 9 10 8 6 4 2

Paper used in the production of this book is a natural, recyclable product
made from wood grown in sustainable forests. The manufacturing process
conforms to the environmental regulations of the country of origin.

Printed in China by Leo Paper Products Ltd.

Acknowledgements
Inside cover notes written by Karra McFarlane

Contents

Chapter 1
Roll Up, Roll Up!

The Big Top Academy is the best school in the world.

The children who go there don't do sums or reading or ordinary things like that. No, the children who go to the Big Top Academy learn how to do brilliant things like juggle plates or fly on a trapeze or dance on a tightrope high above the sawdust ring. Wouldn't you like to go to the Big Top Academy instead of your school?

Lola did not want to go to the Big Top Academy. It was her very first day and she was nervous.

"My tummy hurts," she told her mum as they got close to the school's enormous red and yellow circus tent.

"That's just nerves," Mum said with a kind smile. "You're going to be fine. Don't forget I was even younger than you when I took my first steps on a tightrope."

"But—"

Mum pointed to a giant poster. "You are a Flying Flamingo, Lola, a member of the most famous tightrope-walking family in the world! You were born to do it."

It was true – both Lola's parents were tightrope walkers. Her sister was a tightrope walker. Her grandparents were tightrope walkers, although these days Grandpa carried a walking stick to help him balance.

The Flying Flamingos had performed in every country you could think of, in front of kings and queens and prime ministers and presidents. But none of that made Lola feel any better.

She stepped though the flap of the tent and gazed around. There were rows and rows of empty seats around the sawdust-filled circus ring.

Inside it, a strongman was showing off his muscles to a group of children by lifting a heavy weight. Not far from him was a brightly dressed clown with an orange nose and a big red smile. He tooted a large horn and immediately tripped over his own gigantic feet, which made Lola giggle.

Overhead, she saw someone flying on a trapeze, like a beautiful blue and silver bird. And beneath that there was a lady balancing on a tightrope, holding an umbrella and reading a book as she walked.

"Look," Lola's mum said, waving. "There's Ferdie. I expect she'll be your teacher."

Ferdie looked up from her book and bowed. Lola gulped. How could anyone read and walk a tightrope at the same time? Lola didn't think she could do more than one thing at once, let alone on such a high-up wire.

It might hurt if she fell off; she could even break a bone. And she couldn't help noticing that there was no group of children around Ferdie. No one else was foolish enough to learn how to walk the tightrope.

A man in a scarlet red coat and a gleaming top hat hurried over. "Ah, Madame Flamingo, so lovely to see you!" His twirly black moustache quivered as he smiled. "And welcome, Lola. My name is Rollo and I am the ringmaster here. Are you ready to become a Big Top superstar?"

"Um …" Lola didn't know what
to say.

"But of course you are," Rollo said,
with another toothy smile. "You're a
Flying Flamingo!"

"I suppose so," Lola said, trying to
stop her voice from wobbling.

"Excellent!" Rollo said. "Come on in and join the fun."

Lola hugged her mother extra hard as she said goodbye. Then she followed Rollo into the ring. He patted her on the shoulder. "You are joining us at a very exciting time. We're putting on a show tomorrow. All the parents are coming to watch!"

"Oh!" Lola exclaimed, feeling even more anxious. "I don't know if I can walk the tightrope yet."

Rollo laughed. "I am sure you will be magnificent – with your fabulous family, how could you be anything else?"

Lola hoped he was right. She gazed around the ring. The children were sitting in groups surrounding all the other teachers, watching them perform. Sometimes, a child would get up and join in. Lola liked the clown the best; she thought juggling looked like fun. No one in her family could juggle. They were too busy balancing.

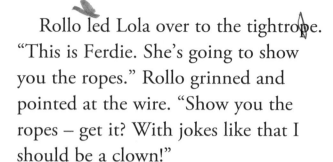

Rollo led Lola over to the tightrope. "This is Ferdie. She's going to show you the ropes." Rollo grinned and pointed at the wire. "Show you the ropes – get it? With jokes like that I should be a clown!"

Lola did her best to smile. "Ha ha ha."

Ferdie groaned. "Rollo, with jokes like that you should be embarrassed." She smiled down at Lola. "Hello little Flamingo. Ready to get started?"

Lola swallowed hard. Up close, the tightrope was even higher than she'd thought. "Um …"

"Of course she is," Rollo cried. "She's going to be the star of the show!"

Lola felt her tummy flip-flop as Rollo walked away. How was she supposed to be a tightrope walker when she was secretly scared of heights?

Chapter 2
Clowning Around

"I don't have to go on to the tightrope straight away, do I?" Lola asked Ferdie, hoping she didn't sound as frightened as she felt.

"Of course not," Ferdie said. "Let's start with something nearer to the ground."

Ferdie climbed down the ladder and placed a plank of wood on top of two upside-down buckets. Lola gazed at it for a moment, then sighed and put on the special leather shoes her mother had given her that morning.

"Stretch your arms out to the sides,"
Ferdie told her as Lola stepped carefully
on to the plank. "Now walk to the
other end."

Frowning hard, Lola did as she was
told. She was surprised to discover it
was easier than she had expected. All
she had to do was put one foot in front
of the other, not too fast and not too
slow, and use her arms to balance.

Some of the other children and their teachers stopped what they were doing to watch. When she reached the halfway point, Lola began to smile. Maybe she was a Flying Flamingo after all.

Then disaster struck. An enormous bang exploded nearby. It made Lola jump and lose her balance. She started to wave her arms in big circles, wobbling this way and that as she struggled to stay upright. And then, almost in slow motion, she felt herself topple backwards. She landed on the ground with a bump and a huge puff of sawdust.

Nobody spoke. Then a loud, wheezy laugh filled the air. Lola looked up to see the clown bent over double, hooting with glee. The children next to him were trying not to laugh. Even Ferdie seemed to be smiling, although she stopped when she saw Lola watching her.

Lola jumped to her feet, her face pink with embarrassment. "At least now I look like a flamingo," she thought, "even if I'm not anywhere near as graceful."

"Are you hurt, Lola?" Ferdie asked.

Lola shook her head – luckily, the sawdust had been super soft. "What was that noise?"

Ferdie glanced over at the clown, who straightened up. "That was Giggles, I'm afraid. He can't resist a joke."

Giggles grinned at Lola and held up his hands. In one of them, she saw what was left of a bright red balloon, and in the other there was a pin.

"Oh!" Lola said. "That wasn't nice."

"But it was funny," Giggles told her, his big red mouth growing even wider than before.

Ferdie muttered under her breath and pointed to the plank again. "This time there'll be no distractions," she said, sending a grumpy look towards Giggles.

Taking a deep, nervous breath, Lola climbed on to the wooden beam. She did her best to concentrate but she couldn't help keeping one eye on Giggles as he clowned around on the other side of the ring.

"It looks like a lot of fun," she decided, as she edged her way along the wood. "Why couldn't my family be clowns instead of tightrope walkers?"

"Bravo!" Ferdie cried, clapping her hands, and Lola realized she'd made it all the way along the plank. "Now it's time to make things harder."

She handed Lola a long pole. Lola knew exactly what to do – she'd seen her sister walk the tightrope balancing a pole plenty of times – but that didn't mean it was easy.

And if it was this tricky on the plank of wood, how much harder would it be when she was up on the tightrope itself?

Lola shivered at the thought, and the pole trembled too. One end dipped and the other swung up, just as Rollo was passing by. It caught the brim of his gleaming top hat, sending it twirling into the air.

It hung there for a moment, then tumbled down and landed neatly on Lola's head!

Laughter filled the Big Top tent.

Cringing with embarrassment, Lola tugged the hat off her head and gave it back to Rollo. "Sorry," she mumbled.

"Not at all," Rollo said, chuckling. "Accidents happen."

Giggles came over and shook Lola's hand. "Amazing!" he exclaimed. "Come and see me if you ever get tired of walking the tightrope. I think you've got funny bones! You'd make a very good clown."

"The trouble is I'm not meant to be funny," Lola thought. "The trouble is I am meant to be a Flying Flamingo. And they're not funny at all. What am I going to do?"

Chapter 3
Red Nose Day

Ferdie gave Lola an umbrella to hold instead of a pole and by lunchtime, Lola could walk from one end of the plank to the other without falling off.

"Excellent work, little Flamingo," Ferdie exclaimed, clapping her hands. "Keep this up and you'll be dancing along the tightrope tomorrow! Your parents will be very proud."

Lola didn't eat much lunch. She sat all on her own with her sandwiches, trying to ignore the squiggly sensation in her tummy.

But every time she thought about performing in the show, her insides squirmed even more. How could she tell Ferdie she was too scared to climb up the ladder to the high wire? How could she tell her family?

With a heavy sigh, she went back to the Big Top to practise walking along the wooden beam. The tent was completely empty; everyone else was still at lunch. Lola didn't look at the high wire. She picked up Giggles the Clown's horn instead and squeezed the end. It made a funny parp sound.

Smiling, Lola pressed it harder. Parp. As well as the horn, there was a box of clown costumes. Lola pulled out a round hat with a floppy flower on it. She put a curly blue wig on her head and jammed the hat on top. Then she squeezed the horn again. Parp parp.

"Try on a red nose," a voice said. "My dad says a clown is never properly dressed without one."

Lola jumped in surprise and turned around. There was a boy watching her from the very back seats. She snatched the hat off her head and blushed.
"I didn't know you were there."

The boy stood up. "I'm Max," he said, walking towards Lola. "Giggles the Clown is my dad."

Now that he was closer, Lola remembered seeing him juggling with the other trainee clowns earlier that morning. "I'm Lola," she said. "I'm—"

"A Flying Flamingo," Max interrupted. "I know."

Lola glanced up at the tightrope and sighed. "Except that I'm not a very good one."

Max smiled. "I thought you did really well. Tightrope walking isn't as easy as it looks."

"Especially when you're scared of heights."

"Oh no!" Max exclaimed. "Do your parents know?"

Lola shook her head. She'd been scared of heights for as long as she could remember but she had never told anyone. Until now. "I don't think they'd understand," she said. "They just expect me to be as brilliant as they are."

"I know exactly how you feel," Max said. "My dad hasn't ever asked if I want to be a clown. He just told me I was."

"Really?" Lola said, staring at him. "What would you like to be?"

Max glanced up at the tightrope. "I want to be a Flamingo."

Just then Ferdie appeared at the entrance to the Big Top. "There you are, Little Miss Flamingo!" she cried. "Are you ready to try the tightrope?"

Lola dropped the wig and hat back into the box with the other clown clothes. "I suppose so," she sighed, trudging over to the ladder.

"The ground looks so far away!" Lola thought as she reached the top.

Ferdie was already on the tightrope in front of her, holding out a hand and smiling. "The trick is not to look down."

Lola squeezed her eyes almost shut. "The trick is not to fall off," she thought, as she took her teacher's hand.

Stretching her other arm out to the side, Lola stepped on to the rope.

After the tiniest of wobbles, she balanced perfectly. "This isn't so bad," she thought in amazement. "Maybe I can do it after all!" She took another step, and another.

"Excellent work!" Ferdie called, letting go of Lola's hand to clap.

For a moment, nothing changed. Then Lola felt herself leaning to the left. Panicking, she pushed her weight to the right – but that only made things worse. She waved her arms in huge circles. Under her feet, the tightrope started to sway and Ferdie began to wobble too.

"Stop!" Ferdie shouted but it was too late.

"Aaaargh!" Lola cried as she fell off.

The harness saved her. It was attached to the top of the tent on a long rope, and it swung her around in an enormous loop. She spotted Max's astonished face below her as she spun above him.

Then she saw Ferdie had tumbled off too – she was flying towards her from the opposite direction. Her rope tangled with Lola's and they twirled around and around and around until they came to a stop, hanging upside down.

Beneath them, Giggles the Clown started to laugh.

Ferdie managed a weak smile. "I'm not sure you're ready for the high wire yet, Lola. Why don't we go back to the plank?"

Chapter 4
Flamingos a Go-Go

Lola found it hard to sleep that night.
She dreamed that Rollo made her wear
a big red wig which fell over her eyes
just as she stepped on to the tightrope,
causing her to boing around the ring like
a kangaroo, with Giggles honking his
horn and pointing.

In the morning, Lola's mother gave her a beautiful pink flamingo outfit.

"You can wear this at the show this afternoon," Mum said. "It's going to be so wonderful to see you walk the tightrope! The whole family is coming to watch."

"Great," Lola said faintly, trying not to imagine her mother's face if she repeated yesterday's performance. "Mum ... do I have to be a Flying Flamingo?"

But her mother wasn't listening. "And your Great Uncle Maldini says he's coming too, if he can escape from the Jaws of Death in time. It's so exciting!"

"But Mum—" Lola tried again.

"Everyone is very proud of you, Lola," her mother finished, giving her arm a little squeeze. "We can't wait for you to join the family business. Now, was there something you wanted to say?"

Lola gave up. "No, Mum."

Ferdie had a determined look on her face when she saw Lola. "I have had an idea," she announced, and whipped out two bright pink umbrellas. "One in each hand!"

Lola exchanged a worried look with Max. "I'm not sure that's going to work."

"Of course it will," Ferdie cried. "You are a—"

"Flying Flamingo," Lola and Max said at exactly the same time. They grinned at each other.

Ferdie smiled too. "Correct. And one way or another, there will be a Flamingo on the tightrope in the show this afternoon."

She turned away and strode towards the ladder.

"Good luck," Max whispered as Lola trailed after Ferdie. "I'd tell you to break a leg but knowing your luck, you probably would!"

Lola tried her hardest to balance on the rope all morning. The problem was that it was so much easier to fall off, even with the help of Ferdie's double umbrellas. In fact, if there'd been such a thing as tightrope faller-offer, Lola would have been top of the class. But of course there wasn't, and by lunchtime, even Ferdie looked wild-eyed and worried.

"No one will let me teach their
children again," she moaned, mopping
her sweaty forehead. "And why should
they when I could not even teach a
Flamingo to walk the tightrope?"

Rollo strode into the centre of the
ring and clapped his hands twice. "The
show will begin at one o'clock," he said,
his moustache bristling with excitement.
"I'm sure I don't need to remind you
that our audience will expect nothing
but the best. This is your time to shine!"

Lola didn't dare look at Ferdie. She wasn't going to shine; she was about to become the biggest joke the Big Top Academy had ever seen. What on earth was she going to do?

Over lunch, Lola thought about running away. "Most people run away to join the circus," she thought, "not the other way around." But running away didn't seem like the right thing to do when her whole family was coming to see her. She trudged into the dressing room to pull on her new flamingo costume.

She had just fastened the long pink feathers into her hair when she heard a strange sound.

"Psssst!"

Lola looked around.

"Psssssst!"

With a puzzled frown, she poked her head around the door of the dressing room and found herself face-to-face with Max, who was dressed from head to toe as a clown.

He thrust a bundle of multicoloured clothes into her arms and handed her a red nose. "I've got an idea," he said. "Why don't you dress up as a clown?"

Lola stared at him. "That's silly. I'll never be able walk the tightrope in those enormous shoes."

"I don't mean that," Max said. "Why don't you dress up as a clown and join me in the ring? Then everyone will see you've got funny bones and they might let you be a clown instead of a tightrope walker."

"Oh!" Lola exclaimed. "I'm not sure I can—"

"Of course you can," Max cut in. "My dad said you were funny, didn't he?"

But that had all been an accident, Lola wanted to tell Max. She couldn't make people laugh on purpose.

Could she?

Chapter 5
Splat!

Max had thought of everything. He'd
even brought some face paints, so
that Lola could give herself a clown
makeover. By the time she'd covered her
face in thick white paint and had pulled
on a crazy green wig, she almost didn't
recognize herself. She added a red nose
and last of all she slipped her feet into a
pair of clumpy yellow shoes.

The band burst into music, signalling the start of the show.

Rollo's voice boomed through the speakers. "Roll up, roll up, for the greatest show in town!"

The other trainee clowns were waiting beside the ring.

"Remember, there's no water in the buckets, just confetti," Max whispered. "And if you fall over, make it look funny!"

The acrobats were on first. Lola watched in amazement as the children rolled and tumbled around the ring. Then it was the strongman and his pupils – it looked like hard work lifting all the heavy weights and Lola was glad Max hadn't suggested she join in with them.

Even so, she grew more and more nervous as the seconds ticked by. What if Giggles was wrong and she didn't have funny bones?

The strongman finished his routine. Then the band began to play a tune Lola recognized – the clown music.

"Here we go," Max said, grabbing some juggling balls. "It's show time!"

Taking a deep breath, Lola followed. The first thing she noticed was how hot and bright the lights were.

She was so busy squinting at them that she didn't watch where she was putting her feet and tripped over her enormous shoes. As she tumbled forwards, she tucked her chin down and turned it into a neat forward roll. The crowd cheered and Lola felt some of her nerves disappear. Maybe she could do this after all …

Spotting a bucket, she hurried towards it. Sure enough, it was filled with hundreds of tiny bits of tissue paper. She picked it up and glanced around, wondering who to pour it over. Then she saw Max bending over and she tiptoed towards him. The audience cheered as she raised it up high ... but she lost her grip at the very last second and the confetti gushed over her own head instead.

Laughter filled the tent. Max turned around and laughed too, holding his tummy with larger-than-life glee. Blowing bits of tissue paper from her face, Lola looked around for another bucket. The plastic ones had all been taken but there was one more, a big red metal bucket at the very edge of the ring. She picked it up and swung it towards Max.

There was a loud splash.

Lola froze. "That didn't sound like confetti," she thought, and peered at Max. To her horror, he was dripping wet. She glanced down at the bucket in her hand – only now did she see the word 'FIRE' painted in big letters on the side. It wasn't part of the clown routine at all – it was a bucket of water in case anything caught fire!

The crowd roared with laughter. Lola
stared at Max. Water was sploshing off
his nose in big fat drops. He winked at
her, then raised his fist and shook it,
as though he was cross. Grinning, Lola
ran off as fast as her clown shoes would
carry her.

In the centre of the ring, she could see the other clowns filling paper plates with creamy custard, to make custard pies. She swept one up as she sped by. "Max must be right behind me," she thought. "If I turn around, I might just be able to plant my custard pie firmly on his face …"

Lola screeched to a stop, sending the sawdust flying. She turned, ready to slap custard into Max's face, but at the very last second she saw a pie flying towards her. She ducked and the plate zoomed over her head.

There was a loud splat and more laughter, although Lola didn't have time to see where the pie had landed because Max was aiming another one at her. She ducked again and got her own plate ready. As she stood up, she aimed for Max's red nose. The custard splatted against his face at exactly the same moment his pie hit Lola's.

The band finished playing with a
flourish and the crowd roared and
howled. Lola wiped the custard from
her eyes and peered out to see everyone
was on their feet – a standing ovation!
Max grabbed her hand and lifted it high
before sweeping low into a bow.

Rollo stepped forwards and waved towards Lola. "Ladies and gentlemen, boys and girls, I am sure you will agree that this clown is the most hilarious of them all!"

He beamed at her; then his black bushy eyebrows beetled into a frown. Reaching out, he pulled the soggy red nose from her face.

Chapter 6
Laughing Lola and
Magnificent Max

"Lola?" Rollo thundered, his face a strange mixture of astonishment and anger. "Aren't you supposed to be walking the tightrope?"

The crowd went quiet. Lola suddenly wished the sawdust would swallow her up. Pretending to be a clown had seemed like such a good idea when Max had suggested it, and she'd had ever so much fun. But now she was looking into Rollo's amazed eyes, it felt like the worst idea ever.

"I didn't mean to make you cross," she said in a quavering voice. "It's just that … well, I don't really like walking the tightrope."

There was a loud gasp somewhere in the crowd and a thud that sounded very much as though someone had fainted.

Lola carried on. "I'm not very good at it and I'm a little bit scared of heights."

Another gasp filled the air, followed by another thud.

"What I really like is making people laugh," Lola said, as a huge drop of custard slid from her wig and plopped on to her shoes. "So we thought if I could show you how funny I could be, you might let me be a clown."

Ferdie hurried into the ring, her face pale. "But … but … you are a Flying Flamingo!"

Lola shook her head. "I'm not. I might be a Flamingo on the outside but inside …" She took her red nose from Rollo and jammed it back on to her face. "I'm Laughing Lola."

There was a third gasp, followed by whispering and muttering among the crowd. Lola didn't dare look up – her family must be so disappointed in her.

Max stepped forwards. "You have to admit Lola was a great clown. Even if she did throw the wrong bucket over me."

"Sorry," Lola said.

Giggles nodded. "But it was funny. I think Lola was born to be a clown."

And then there was a clattering noise, as though several people were hurrying down from the stands. Lola looked up to see her mother and father climbing into the ring.

"Lola, is it true?" Mum asked. "Are you really afraid of heights?"

Lola nodded. "I'm sorry. I know you want me to be a tightrope walker like the rest of the family."

Mum took her hands. "We've got plenty of tightrope walkers. But we don't have anyone who can make us laugh."

"But I thought you wanted me to be a Flying Flamingo, just like you?" Lola said.

Dad shook his head. "What we want most of all is for you to be happy. And I'm sure Granny and Grandpa will feel the same way, once they've woken up and got over the shock."

Mum smiled. "Great Uncle Maldini is delighted. He says he's always felt a bit left out among all of us Flamingos."

Rollo clapped, his twirly moustache bustling. "It's a deal, then – Lola will join the circus as our newest star clown!"

"But what about me?" Ferdie complained. "I don't have anyone to teach."

Lola stared hard at Max.

Slowly, he raised his hand. "I've always wanted to walk the tightrope."

He kicked off his clown shoes and climbed the ladder to the high wire. Clipping on the safety harness, he walked carefully along the tightrope as though he had been doing it all his life.

Lola looked around and spotted the juggling balls. "Max!" she called, and threw them to him one by one.

Max caught them and began to juggle as he walked. The crowd clapped and Ferdie looked like she might explode with delight.

"Max is a Flying Flamingo," Lola said. "No, wait – he's Magnificent Max!"

Rollo turned to Giggles. "What do you think?" he said eagerly. "Can Max be our star tightrope walker instead of a clown?"

Everyone held their breath. For a moment, Giggles looked like he might say no. Then he smiled. "Of course he can."

"Then Laughing Lola and Magnificent Max shall both have their wish," Rollo boomed. "At the Big Top Academy, we make everyone's dreams come true!"

Max and Lola beamed with delight as everyone began to cheer. Lola felt a bubble of happiness fizz in her tummy and she opened her mouth to let it out.

Well, with a name like Laughing Lola she couldn't really do anything else.

About the author

Who doesn't love the circus? If someone could magically grant me a talent, I'd like to be able to walk the tightrope or fly on the trapeze in a beautiful sparkly costume. But I think I'm probably better at making people laugh – I love writing funny books. And I can already spin plates, make balloon animals and lick my own elbow (try it!). So I think I'd probably be a brilliant clown, just like Laughing Lola.